IN PRAISE OF
LIFE MATTERS, SO LET'S EAT LIKE IT!

"Jabez is not an influencer. He is a world changer. He is not a talker but he is an executor. Most people speak about their dreams but Jabez is living his and teaching others how to live theirs through taking their health seriously. His selfless acts for humanity and positive electric innerg has led him to inspire billions of others to live their dreams as well. Not only does Jabez encourage people to develop a wealthy mind but he inspires them to have a healthy heart by encouraging them, not waiting until their near death to see the value in living. Your greatest wealth is your health. Jabez is walking people out of darkness into the light by shining brightness on them through educating them about their health. Jabez will definitely shift your mindset from being on a DIEt to being on a LIVE IT!"

Billionaire P.A., World Changer, Founder/CEO of Wealthy Minds, Inc.

"I've been following Jabez on the social media app Tik Tok and was enamored by his personality and his desire to impact millions of lives to take care of their bodies. Before following Jabez, I didn't pay too much attention to the things that I was

buying in the grocery store. I now find myself looking at ingredients and putting things back on the shelves that aren't in alignment with my health goals. Life Matters, So Let's Eat Like It is a timely book for all people who are looking to regain control of their bodies through an effective and easy guide. Your body will thank you after reading this book. Enjoy your journey!"

Tony Shavers III, Best-Selling author of Is Your DREAM Really Worth It? Discover Your Passion, Purpose, and Plan

"Served by a God..."

"You are what you think, says the first brain. And you become what you eat, says the second brain. This book teaches one to be mindful of what we ingest because that's an investment in the health of your life and since health is wealth, your gut must be fed the best in what rejuvenates, reinvigorates and reenergises it on a daily. Please don't let this collect dust in your book collection. This is a living book. So read it and start practicing it. Brother Jabez did an excellent job in human service here..."

Hakeem Anderson-Lesolang,
Your Go-To Holistic Transformational Therapist (cHT, RTT)
2x Best Selling Author (200 Truths About Love & in Rosewater)

"As quoted by Hippocrates "Let food be thy medicine and medicine be thy food". Jabez has secured his spot amongst the greats by curating a modern day novel that guides one to LIFE! Millions of dollars are poured into Food & beverage marketing campaigns however the ingredients come in the smallest print possible. Hmmm why is that? Well Jabez delivered a stellar must read with this book & I'd recommend this to Family, Friends, co-workers and anyone looking to enjoy their time on this earth in full health and strength. Unlike Jabez's Health books, there is no sequel to this LIFE we live. Each food consumption should come from a clear & calculated mind."

Justin Obida, Founder of Crypto Money Team,
Galadima to the Lakweme People, Gombe State NG

LIFE

MATTERS

S O   L E T ' S

LIKE IT!

A Priceless Guide to Attain
Your Natural Body Size.

JABEZ EL ISRAEL

TABLE OF CONTENTS

DEDICATION

This book is dedicated to my family—Nicole, Shaniya, Jacinda, Budda, Supreme, and Mekhi. You guys are my why and I love you deeply!

FOREWORD

THE FIRST TIME I MET Jabez, I noticed his vibrant energy. You can't help it. Like someone who was born to cheer you on, he radiates enthusiasm for everything he does and everyone with whom he interacts. Which is a blessing for us all, because Jabez's energy isn't limited to his voice or his body—it finds its way into his writing, too. The book you hold in your hands goes beyond useful: it's the encouraging wake-up call you've been looking for on your health journey.

Despite our advances in technology and hyper connectivity through the internet, it's easy for simple knowledge to escape us, like what we should eat. Whether we're trapped by inherited family habits or frustrated by conflicting messages from experts, eating no longer feels like an opportunity to gather with loved ones and be nourished. It's become a chore, and a source of contention: we *want* to be healthy, but we don't always know *how*.

Enter *Life Matters, So Let's Eat Like It*. With a realness that feels like talking to your best friend, Jabez finally brings clarity to the confusing world of food. I won't spoil the big reveal, but once you read his simple advice, you'll wonder how you missed it for so long. Healthy eating doesn't have to be an additional task on your to-do list—it can be the reason for newfound delight.

Jabez's physical transformation isn't some lofty story. With heart and humility, his journey feels like it could be anyone's—which means his amazing results can be anyone's, too. Thank you, Jabez, for bringing your experience and life energy to us in this book. And thank you for making health feel like something we can all achieve. This book is full of revelations and encouragement I intend to savor for a long time.

Laura Thomas

Founder of Next Level Story, speaker, and author of

The Magic of Well-Being: A Modern Guide to Lasting Happiness

INTRODUCTION

I WAS THINKING OF TITLING this book *Black Lives Matter, So Let's Eat Like it*, but I changed my mind because I feel like this topic is for anybody who may benefit from it. With that being said, I want to express this: My heart is actually deeply connected to the "Black" community in America. In my opinion, we're the ones who need the most guidance out of all of the different races in America. I think it's important to know that the inspiration for this book came from a desire to help out the African American community in America. But interestingly enough, as this book was being created, I began to get an overwhelming feeling that the messages are not only for the "Black" community, but for anyone in the world who is overweight, unhealthy, lacking energy, and/or unhappy.

My spirit has always desired to help the people around me. I used to help people even when it hurt me. I honestly cared more about the people around me than I did about myself. Then something fantastic happened! I had an epiphany about eight years ago that I had to help myself before I could REALLY help others. And I realized that the first thing I had to do was clean my body in order to clean my mind.

I believe that the first step to true happiness starts with the conscious decision to eat healthy. Not just for a while, but to eat healthy for the rest of your life! In order to be happy we have to be healthy, and in order to stay healthy we have to eat correctly. This book is a guide to do just that. It is designed to make it easy for people to know what to eat and what to stay away from.

Growing up in America, I've realized that there's a major problem in the way we eat food. We've been taught to eat three meals a day and go to the grocery store or restaurant (oftentimes fast food) to get our food. The problem is most of us were not taught to read the ingredients on the back of the pack. It was not explained to us that, when choosing an option at a restaurant, we can ask the server specifics about the ingredients used in whatever meal we are considering.

For the most part, we just kind of follow behind our parents and peers and the way they eat. Basically, monkey see monkey do. The thing is people only know what they've been exposed to, and we don't know what we haven't been exposed to. Like the saying goes, you don't know what you don't know. Because of this, the food choices the average American citizen is making is a modern-day catastrophe!

This book has been constructed to make health and diet extremely easy to understand. Unfortunately, in America, these subjects are overcomplicated big time!

This is a short book. It is designed to be a very easy read and extremely valuable. To explain how valuable it is, I'll use an analogy: It's like the difference between $20 million in cash with all $20 bills. Think about how much space all of that cash takes up. Then compare that to a $20-million diamond and how much space that takes up. They're both worth $20 million. One just takes up a lot less space. The same is true with this book. It's not a big book like one you'd get studying in college. It's going to be a very simple book but extremely valuable!

The amazing thing is you could sum this entire book up in a couple of statements: Natural versus unnatural and high vibration versus low vibration.

So, as you read this book, I need you to put in the forefront of your mind that the principles and how-tos of this book (if practiced) will change your life forever!

CHAPTER ONE

BACK STORY OF MY LIFE

T O SUM UP MY LIFE, I've lived amongst many different cultures. My mom is white from Cumberland, Wisconsin and my dad is Black from Miami, Florida. I was born in Cumberland, Wisconsin in 1983. Between my birth and the age of seven I lived in Cumberland, Wisconsin, Minneapolis, Minnesota, and Fairbanks, Alaska. My mom and dad divorced when I was a baby. So I moved around between family members until I was adopted by my mom's brother and his wife. Shout out to Butch and Julie. I love you guys and I appreciate everything that you've done for me! I lived with them between the ages of seven and 15 in La Center, Washington and attended La Center High school (which was an all-white school). By the age of 15 I was able to experience all those different areas. I took part in the ways they were living and eating.

Then I moved in with my mom in Los Angeles, California. I lived there for about a year. I went to Taft High School for one semester. It was a blessing because I was able to experience the Los Angeles culture, which was way different than the places I had lived previously.

After that, I moved to Miami, Florida midway through my junior year in high school, and I graduated from Coral Gables, class of 2001. Here's a side-note: I actually came out of high school the same year as Frank Gore. We played on the same football team at Coral Gables High School. I would like to take this opportunity to congratulate him on all of his success in the NFL. He is the hardest working and most talented running back I have ever seen in my life! You deserve everything you've achieved, my brother!

After high school, I received a full-ride scholarship to play football at FIU. I was able to see the college culture intertwined with the culture of being a student athlete.

I was extremely active living this type of lifestyle, being young and playing sports. I played basketball, ran track, and played football throughout high school, so I was always exercising and using a lot of energy. This same active lifestyle carried into my college life. It's important to note that I was eating the same way as the people around me and not thinking twice about it. For example, I would order off the value section at fast-food restaurants for a cheap meal. I bought white bread for sandwiches. Basically, I based my food choices on what I saw the people around me eating. From those examples, I chose the foods that tasted the best to me.

I played football at FIU until my junior year when my scholarship was revoked because I failed a drug test twice. At that time, I had a habit of smoking weed on a consistent basis. I was also selling enough of it that word was getting around and there were people who felt like I wasn't a good influence on the team.

Even though I was a good-hearted person, looking back, I now know that I was not the right type of influence for a successful athletic program. I've also realized that, at that time, my heart wasn't really in athletics either.

After college, I moved back to Coconut Grove with my grandmother for a little bit. Then, I got my own place and started my path as a salesman, taking care of myself and my bills. A lot happened in this period of my life, but the most important was the birth of my first child, Jacinda.

Interestingly, when I think back on it, I adopted a philosophy of eating once a day during this period of my life, due to not having much money. Because I wanted to save money, I ate less. Overtime, I got used to it, and it was easy to just eat once a day. I did that for a few years. Then I got into a relationship with my wife, Nicole, in 2010.

I began to make more money and got comfortable. I started exercising less. I was still eating the same way as before, but I just ate more of the same type of food. I remember being taught by my grandma that a complete meal was meat, starch (rice, potatoes, or pasta), and a vegetable. So most of the meals I cooked were meat, a starch, and a canned vegetable. If I did go out to eat, the majority of time it was fast food. After doing this for a few years, I began to put on weight. As I was getting older (between the ages of 28 and 32), I gained around 80 pounds. Eventually, I was all the way up to about 260 pounds when my natural size is around 160!

Around the age of 32, something happened that I will never forget. My wife and I were in the Bedroom one night, and suddenly she looked at me and chuckled, then poked at my chest saying, "Damn bae, you got titties!" Lol! I can laugh now, but at the time, it wasn't funny; yet it was very true. My gut was getting big! I would get sweat underneath my gut and sweat underneath my chest. I had noticed the change happening in my body, but I was kind of in denial about it until she said that. It made me decide that I had to do something. I knew I had to make some changes!

I remember walking into the bathroom full of emotions. I looked into the mirror and had an epiphany that changed my life. I realized when I was looking into the mirror that I was holding my gut in to make myself look skinnier. I did this automatically without even trying to. I realized in that moment that I was lying to myself every time I looked in the mirror. I did not like what I was seeing, so I was holding my stomach in to change the way I appeared to myself. I remember realizing this and deciding that I would stop lying to myself. I decided in that moment to relax my body and take an HONEST look at myself. This moment was LIFE CHANGING! While I was looking at myself, I made an intentional choice to NEVER eat fast food again. At that time, I was eating fast food literally four to seven days a week. I believed that fast food was the cause of me being so overweight. The year was 2014. I was so intentional about that decision that I haven't eaten fast food to this day! Needless to say, I started losing weight. Over a period of three to six months, I lost around thirty pounds. Then something strange happened. To my surprise, I stopped losing weight. I went from 260 pounds down to 230, then about four months passed with me staying at 230 pounds. Honestly, I was starting to get discouraged. Then a miracle happened! I came across VALUABLE information that I chose to put to practice. This intentional choice put me on a path to getting back down to my natural body size while still eating the food I liked!

CHAPTER TWO

THE CONFUSION AROUND DIET IN AMERICA

BEFORE I GET INTO THE key points of this chapter, I would like to talk about the confusion around diet in America. America has so many different diets to try that it's hard to know where to start. There's the keto diet, the Atkins diet, and you'll also hear about seven-day challenges. I remember Jenny Craig commercials being on TV all the time when I was younger. The list goes on and on. All of these options come with sales pitches that sound like, "Get down to your swimsuit size," or, "Get your summer body right." Most

17

of these diets are presented and sold as a temporary outcome. The final goal is for you to get to your optimum weight rather than making a permanent healthy lifestyle change so you never put on that same weight again.

A part of me believes this dynamic evolved so that the diet companies can keep making money from the same customers. If a customer is instead sold on the idea of making a permanent lifestyle change, once they make that change, they won't need the diet company again. Permanent change doesn't continue making these companies money.

Now, about the VALUABLE information. I knew even before I came across it that I had to make a lifestyle change. I knew that I had to make a decision and stick to it for life. At that point, I had already decided to start eating only once a day again. Then, I came across this documentary, and its main point was so simple, yet so incredibly effective when applied. It's funny because I've told so many people about this, including my family and people I see on a weekly or daily basis. I tell a lot of people about this one simple thing that you can do. I also tell them that when I did it, I lost 60 pounds. What fascinates me is that most people choose to not apply it to their lives. It also fascinates me that the people who took the advice experienced similar results as me. So, now I'm telling you that if you want to lose the extra weight, you can do so easily. All that you have to do is cut this out of your diet and replace it with something else...

ARE YOU READY??? This is it...

STOP EATING ENRICHED FOOD! I swear they are a product of the devil!

So, what is enriched food? Enriched food is food that is put through the enrichment process. The most common products are flour, rice, bread (made with flour) and pasta (made with flour).

Whoever coined the term "enriched" is brilliant, in a scary way! "Enriched" sounds like a good thing, but really it means stripping the flour or rice of all its nutritional value and leaving an empty shell—often bleached—as the final product. It will fill you up, but it has absolutely no nutritional value. This is why these foods can sit on the shelf forever and not go bad. Anything that is good for you will turn rotten relatively quickly. If something does not turn rotten at a natural pace, that's a sign that it is not good to consume. Our bodies are designed to eat natural foods.

Most often, you'll see enriched products in foods that are made from flour, like bread, pasta, and pastries. A lot of cornmeal and rice are enriched as well. The packaging will always say if it's enriched in the ingredients, and it's usually the first ingredient they name.

But it is important to note that food companies are getting tricky and putting the word "enriched" on other parts of the packaging as well

When you look at the ingredients in a loaf of white bread, you'll see enriched bleached flour. Or, if you look at the ingredients in most packs of pasta, you'll see enriched flour as the first ingredient. Avoid these products like the plague!

Here is the beautiful thing! You don't have to stop eating the foods you love! Just replace them with all-natural options of the same thing. Flour should only have the name of the grain or grains that were used to make it. That's it!

Now, going back to the documentary. It masterfully explained the enrichment process as a chemical process similar to how drugs are made. This process takes all of the nutrients out of the food and leaves in empty products. They explained how the body automatically turns the food into fat because it assumes that you're eating everything that you can get your hands on in order to get ready for a long winter with very little food. Your body thinks that you're trying to store fat so that it can use it as fuel to make it through the winter.

I've searched everywhere for the name of this documentary, and I just could not find it. If anyone believes that they know the film I'm talking about, especially the name of the creators, please notify me. I would really like to meet them and to personally thank them.

While I was watching this documentary, I started to think about my eating patterns. I realized that I ate enriched products every day. Pretty much every dinner that I cooked was meat with either enriched white rice or enriched parboiled rice that I cooked in different ways. I would also often cook canned vegetables. At least once a week, I cooked pasta, whether it was to make macaroni and cheese, tuna salad, or spaghetti. Whatever it was, I realized that every time I purchased pasta, it was enriched pasta. If I didn't cook, I usually got fast food. All fast-food restaurants use enriched flour to make their buns for the hamburgers. I was eating enriched products pretty much EVERY day. When I realized this, I made up my mind to stop eating enriched products and replace them with all-natural products. Instead of white rice, I started eating brown rice, sushi rice, wild rice, jasmine rice, emperor's rice, or basmati rice. Instead of white bread, I started eating organic, all-natural wheat bread. Instead of enriched pasta, I replaced it with pasta made with organic whole wheat flour. Instead of fast food, I started eating at restaurants using all-natural recipes.

In this documentary, they also broke down the difference between fresh vegetables and canned vegetables. They explained that because canned vegetables sit in a can for so long, they lose all their nutrients. So, when you eat them, it does basically the same thing as when you consume enriched products. Your body will turn the food into fat to get ready for a long period without eating. So, I made up my mind to stop eating canned vegetables and to eat only fresh vegetables.

I was curious to see if these changes would alter my body weight. I had to know! So I became aware of everything I chose to eat. And I decided to eat all-natural foods for the rest of my life.

What happened next blew my mind and reinforced my belief in eating all-natural foods. Over the next six to nine months, I lost 60 pounds. This was with basically no exercise. The only thing I did differently was go on a walk every day. Even if it was just a quarter mile.

If you commit to this one simple change of replacing enriched products with natural products and canned vegetables with fresh vegetables, you are going to change your life forever...You will also love me like a family member!

I just gave you a diamond right there. Now, some people might read this and say, "I'm sold!" So they choose to commit to making this change. Some people might say, "Yeah, I'm gonna do this!" and they might stick to it for a week or two, then here comes the birthday cake, or here comes that sandwich on white bread or a white sub sandwich. Maybe they'll go to the restaurant and order their favorite pasta and forget to ask the server if they have pasta that's made with natural flour.

The point that I'm trying to make is that we are creatures of habit. Anytime we make changes like this, it takes self-discipline and self-awareness on a daily basis. In other words, you have to be conscious of everything that you put into your mouth every day for this to work for you.

The great news is that if you've made it this far in the book, you are serious about making changes in your life. You really want to see changes in your body. At this point, it is a simple choice that you have to make, and you have to hold yourself accountable. If and when you do, your life will be changed forever, which brings us to our next chapter, and, in my opinion, the most important chapter in this book…Mindset.

CHAPTER THREE

MINDSET

GOING INTO ANY LIFESTYLE CHANGE, you have to have the right mindset first. This is very important because everything that I told you in the last chapter will truly change your life! You will be more energetic, you'll be fitter, and you'll lose that extra unwanted weight. I lost 60 pounds from just making this decision, but I was also committed to the decision. My mindset was: I'm doing this not only for me. I'm doing this for my kids because I know that by eating the right foods, I'm going to live a longer life. I'll be there for my kids longer. I'll have more energy, and it's not like I have to stop eating the things that I like. I just have to eat the natural version of the things that I like, as opposed to the unnatural version I've grown accustomed to.

It's incredible how impressionable humans are. When we are unaware of something it's almost as if it's not there. We are unaware of the fact that we have been taught to eat food that tastes good. Most of us choose things to eat strictly based on how they taste. That's as deep as our reflection goes when thinking about the foods we choose to eat. Why weren't we taught in school to eat foods for the energy they give us? Why don't they teach us that there are foods like natural kale, blueberries, turmeric, wild salmon, and organic dark chocolate that actually strengthen our brains, making us smarter? If we had a different mindset about food, and we ate for the benefit of living a longer, healthier life, we would gladly choose different foods. Most of us were never influenced to choose food for health benefits, just taste. When we start choosing food for health, then we can figure out ways to make that food taste amazing. I believe this is the key for everyone looking to lose weight, have more energy, and think clearer in life.

28

When I understood all of the benefits of making this change, it inspired me. It gassed me up! I was juiced up! Listen, I was so excited that I knew what was about to happen because it just made sense. I saw how enriched foods were made and I said to myself, "Am I really putting this into my body?? I'm putting drugs in my body everyday!? I need to stop doing this to myself!" I felt disgusted, and if I continued doing the same thing, I would have been disgusted with myself. At the same time, thinking about making the change and doing the right thing excited me! So, it was at that point when I realized this: I said to myself, "I am going to make this change for life! This isn't a diet. This isn't a situation where I'm going to do this for a while and then go back to my old decision-making." I was not looking at it like, "I really want to eat my white rice. I really want to eat my white bread. It's going to be so hard." I wasn't looking at like that. I was looking at it like there are people out here making poison that kills us slowly. Then they give it to us like it's okay!? I'm getting upset when I think about how they have no morals. They don't have scruples.

These people are profiting from doing this to food before selling it to us and our kids, and they disgust me! I don't want anything to do with the products you people are selling! Now I see clearly. My eyes are open, so now my mindset is in the right place to be committed to this change for life! If you want the results I had, you're going to have to do the same thing...Period!

CHAPTER FOUR

READ THE INGREDIENTS ON THE BACK OF THE PACK

ALRIGHT, NOW HERE'S THE REAL. It's as real as I can get, and it shocks me how few people do this…You need to read the INGREDIENTS on the BACK of the PACK! We already discussed enriched products. Let's take it a step further—but don't worry, this is very simple. When you read the back of the pack and you see long chemical names, these are processed materials. They're going to take corn, soy, wheat (basically different things) from the ground and they're going to chemically alter them. They're

31

going to put something in the food and they're going to label it as a preservative, or they might label it as a coloring agent. They might call it blue 12. Now, when we read red 40, or something like this, that should throw up a red flag! What is red?? You're just going to tell me that you put red in the food and then we just put that sh*t in our mouths with no questions asked? What is red? Is it a red crayon? Is it a red marker? I mean, for real!?

Then, you have to look at the big names like sodium metabisulfite and sulfur dioxide. Another one that I see a lot is dextrose, but the list goes on and on.

Hey, look at the ingredients in your chips. Look at the snacks that you get. Look at the candy, the candy bars. Even the so-called health bars that you eat. Read the ingredients, man! It could say on the packet "zero sugar" and then it has 37 chemicals in it and all that you see on the front of the pack is where it says (in big letters) "SUGAR FREE," and you're like, "Oh, it's healthy! Let me just get this." It's the same thing with diet soda or sugar-free soda. They don't put the chemical sugar in it. They use a different chemicals to sweeten it and then they say it's sugar free. When you drink it, it's still sweet, right? Red flags should be popping up in your brain!

This is what I'm saying: I want you to look at yourself in the mirror. I want you to ask yourself: Do I check the ingredients of what I eat? No exceptions? If the answer is no, then dedicate yourself to reading the ingredients and only eating the foods that have all-natural things listed in the ingredients.

If there's anything in the ingredients that you can't pronounce or you don't recognize, nine out of ten times it's not good for you, so don't eat it. Look for something that is all-natural instead...Simple!

I'll tell you this: If a fruit or vegetable comes from the ground and it has seeds, nine out of ten times it comes from the creator of this planet and our bodies are compatible with it.

Now, also be aware that nowadays you have the genetically modified fruits and vegetables too, and they're getting out of hand, but that's a whole other topic for a whole other book. But I'll tell you this: when you eat the fruits and the vegetables, even if they're genetically modified, it's better than this trash in a pack that takes years to spoil. It's also better than fast food, trust me!

Attention

When you go to grocery store, there's the middle part of the grocery store and there's the outside part of the grocery store that goes around the outside wall. I don't care where you are in America. Grocery stores follow the same floor plan. All of the items in the middle of the floor (in all the aisles)—that's the DANGER ZONE! I'm telling you right now, when you find yourself there, be careful! You are in the danger zone! You'll notice that the stuff around the outside of the store is the vegetables, fruits, and the meats. This is the section from which you want to be picking the majority of your diet.

The million-dollar question

What is the best thing to eat out of the grocery store? First, is fresh fruits, followed by fresh vegetables, natural grains and lastly, unprocessed meat.

Let that sink in…I just gave you another diamond.

Sometimes, the simplest things lead to the biggest results. Most people know that vegetables and fruits are the best things to eat. But how many people actually eat mostly fruits and vegetables? Our bodies were constructed from the same materials of this earth. So, our bodies are most compatible with natural things from this earth. Let me share an analogy to illustrate my point. If you put the wrong oil in a car, that car will start to have problems. Or, if you put diesel gas in a car that takes unleaded gas, that car will stop operating, right? It is the same thing with our bodies. As a culture, we see way too many diseases popping up in our bodies. Almost all diseases can be traced back to the decisions we make when choosing the foods we consume.

Start eating more fruits and vegetables. Eat mostly fresh fruits and vegetables. Some people will say, "Yeah, but vegetables taste nasty to me." Listen, I get it, but this is where we come back to mindset. Ask yourself this: Is it more important for food to taste good than for me to live a healthy, long, and energetic life? A lot of us put more value on the way food tastes rather than on the effect that food will have on our bodies. Remember, food is an energy source. That's its purpose. There is a solution to every problem. If you don't think vegetables taste good, that's because you haven't had them prepared in a way that you like. It's the same with meat and unhealthy food. All that they did was use flavor combinations to make it taste good. Trust me, the same way that you can make unhealthy food taste good, you can make healthy food taste good. Get creative with your culinary mindset. Start looking up different recipes. Google and YouTube are full of recipes and explanations for how to put amazing flavor on healthy food.

You might say, "Well, I like Fruit Loops." Well, guess what? Get the organic brand and read the ingredients! It won't be called Fruit Loops. It will be called something different but taste just like Fruit Loops. Down here in Florida, they have healthy options in Publix. Publix's natural brand is called "Green Wise." They're not going to be as sweet, but you could drop a little bit of natural sweetener on there if it's that important to you. But I promise you this: Everything unhealthy has a healthy replacement. You might like Cinnamon Toast Crunch. Okay, well, read the ingredients on the back of Cinnamon Toast Crunch and then ask yourself— Do you want to keep putting that poison into your temple?

I don't want to get too deep but I'm going to say this: We are all created by the creator of all things. When you look around, you have to pinch yourself. We are on a beautiful planet! At this very moment, I'm speaking into a recorder that's translating the words that I'm saying into the written word. Then, when these written words get in front of your face, you can read the symbols and understand the message that I desire to get to you...Incredible!

How is my body constructed like this? I've been alive for 38 years. I've made three kids out of my loins! I've taken care of five kids! They are beautiful, talented, and smart! I think to move my finger and it moves! I think, move my legs and they move! This body and its capabilities are fantastic! Look at all of the cars on the road or all the beautiful homes that have been constructed worldwide. We can construct all of these things with the elements that are available to us here on this planet. We are a brilliant species. We are truly incredible! Really look at how blessed you are and treat yourself with the respect you deserve! If you don't, your body is going to reflect it. When you look in the mirror, your body is going to scream at you saying, "You've f****** me up! Look at what you're doing to me!" We only have one body to work with and the mirror doesn't lie. If you're overweight, you need to make some changes. Love yourself, embrace the truth, and be set free!

I want to say this to humanity: We are all in this together. When I look around at all of the people on the planet, I feel a connection to everyone. I see you as a brother and as a sister and I want you to know that I love you! But even more importantly, I want you to love yourself and treat yourself with the respect and love that you deserve! You have to love yourself more than the love that you have for the way food tastes. You have to love yourself more than the love that you have for the convenience of prepared, unhealthy food options.

Always remember and remind yourself: Your body is your temple, and you only have one!

Two Diamonds

I'm going to drop two important names right now: Yahki & Yada. Go on YouTube and type in Yahki Awakened Watch his videos. He is a true healer. He has healed hundreds of people from "incurable diseases." What makes it even more impressive is he cures his patience naturally. Another incredible healer is Yada, go on Instagram and look up @yada_awakening. Do yourself a favor and check them out, please. They're going to break down what is healthy and what isn't healthy, masterfully! This book is not about all of the details. This book is about the basics so that anyone who is not aware of this information can get started achieving their natural body size today.

CHAPTER FIVE

FOODS TO AVOID

I N THIS CHAPTER, I'M GOING to discuss foods you want to consider removing from the list of what you eat. With that being said, I highly recommend doing your own research about anything anyone has to say, including me and what I am going to present to you in this chapter.

This year I read the entire Bible from front to back for the first time. Now, this is not a book about spirituality or religion, but I do want to give credit and praise to the creator

LIFE MATTERS, SO LET'S EAT LIKE IT!

of all things, who was referred to in the original Hebrew Bible as YHWH (Yod-Hey-Waw-Heh).

In the Bible, the book of Leviticus goes over diet. Why am I mentioning this? I started practicing what I'm about to present to you because it makes logical sense. What's amazing is that after practicing it, I saw and felt the results!

Because of the amount of bibles that have been sold in the world, it is evident that there's a high percentage of people world-wide who believe there's value within its pages. For these reasons, I feel it is valuable to put this information within the pages of THIS book.

I was very surprised to learn that the book of Leviticus goes over diet. It also goes over hygiene. Within the education of diet and what we should and shouldn't eat, I have precited the rules laid out by the Bible for about a year now.

Because of the results I've had, I am dedicated to practicing them for life. Leviticus describes the benefits of fasting, the benefits of not eating pork, the benefits of not eating any animal with paws, and also points out that we should only eat the flesh of animals with hooves and that "chew of the cud." Chewing of the cud is when animals chew their food, swallow it, bring it back up, and then repeat the cycle. Cows, deer, goats, and lambs are just a few animals that chew of the cud.

Leviticus also goes over what types of birds to avoid and which birds are good to eat. It's also specific about which water animals are good to eat. It is written that we should only eat fish that have scales and fins. Also, it specifies that we should not consume anything that drags its belly on the ground, like lizards, frogs, snakes, and things like this.

Since I've followed this advice, I've noticed my energy increase and I have a better memory. I've also noticed a lot more random blessings in my life. Unexpected things have been happening for me. People from my past are reaching out with opportunities I did not expect. In short, ever since I put the words of Leviticus to practice, my life has gotten noticeably better! Not only for me, but also for the people around me!

I've been saying that I wanted to write a book for over a decade. I think it's more than a coincidence that I'm actually doing it the same year that I took on the philosophy of eating as outlined in Leviticus. I'm recording this book as we speak, and I have a strategy to market it. I'm investing in more things than I have in my entire life, especially knowledge.

I want wisdom. I want to move in a perfect way. Being real with myself is one of my most valuable assets. I wasn't always this way. The longer I consistently ate healthy, the easier it became to face my flaws. I know that I have been lost, and when I look around at humanity, a lot of us are. Many of us are unhealthy, unhappy, and really don't know what to do about it.

Listen to Your Body

The good news is that our body actually communicates with us and shows us what's good for it and what's not good for it. All you have to do is learn how to listen.

A simple way to know if something is good for you is to observe how you feel two hours after you eat. If your energy stays the same or increases, the food that you ate was good for you. It's giving you energy, which is what it's supposed to do. But on the other hand, if you begin to feel tired or sluggish, this is an indication that the food that you ate is taking energy away from you (showing you that the food was not good for your body). You might even feel like laying down and taking a nap out of nowhere. So, when you eat foods that take away your energy, make a mental note and avoid those foods moving forward. Have you ever noticed that greasy, fatty food tastes good but then you get tired afterwards? That's because your body is using so much energy to digest it. That energy can be used for your immune system and/or for burning off unwanted, unnecessary fat. Eating healthy will even provide the extra energy that your body needs in order to automatically go to work, restoring nerve cells and neural pathways in your brain! Your body is a magical, blessed machine with capabilities far beyond what we understand!

In short, ever since I made the decision to practice the guidelines I have laid out in this book, my life has undergone drastic changes for the better. I believe with all my heart that if it worked for me and if you're reading these words right now, it will work for you too. WHEN you put it into practice!

Be Aware

Being aware means simply focusing on truth. Things that we are not aware of are simple things that we haven't focused on. I had a weight problem. I was 100 pounds overweight. I became aware of the fact that I was overweight because of my actions and the choices I'd made. At that point, I started to focus on this truth and look for solutions.

When my mentality shifted, I began to learn what to eat and what not to eat. I became aware of all of the mistakes I had been making years prior, which led to my weight gain.

I started looking into how fast food was produced. I became aware of how unhealthy it is. The ingredients for every item in all fast-food restaurants are available online. All that I did was begin to look at the ingredients of the things that I ate. I was shocked to see how many chemicals, enriched products, and genetically modified foods were included in what I was eating. I was now AWARE, and I made my mind up to stop eating fast food.

I believe we are all aware that fast food is unhealthy. What most of us are not fully aware of is *why* it is so unhealthy. When you look at the ingredients in fast food, and then look up the side effects of these ingredients, you become aware of the problem. Many of these ingredients lead to obesity if over-consumed, cancer, and a wide range of other health problems.

Many of us have lost loved ones to health problems related to what that person was consuming. The interesting thing is that a lot of us did not connect the dots between them dying and what they were consuming. We just see the health problem. Then, many of us don't connect the dots that we are consuming the same things. A lot of us don't connect the dots to the fact that what we choose to eat is literally a life-and-death decision! We are not aware of this because we do not die right away when we eat these things. They kill us slowly over time. This is why I say that the American food industry is pernicious!

Just because we are not aware of something does not mean that thing is not affecting us. At the end of the day, it is up to me to choose to be as aware as possible in life. The same is true for all of us. Also, we need to be aware of the pesticides that are getting sprayed on fruits and vegetables. When you get your fruits and vegetables from the store, there's going to be a sticker with a number on it. It's usually a four-digit number and the first digit will let you know how organic, natural, and pesticide-free that produce is. The lowest first digit is a three and the highest is a nine. Put it like this: the lower the number, the more genetically modified and pesticide-drenched it is. The higher the number, the more organic and natural it is, with fewer pesticides used in the growing process. Do your research…Be aware!

Always wash your fruits and vegetables with water and vinegar. Vinegar helps to remove many harmful chemicals that are in these pesticides. When you wash them well, you'll avoid putting most of these unhealthy chemicals into your system. There's research on the harmful effects of these pesticides, not only on our immune system but also our brain. It is very scary. Please do your own research on this so that you can be truly aware. Don't just take my word for it. Again, wash your fruits and vegetables before you eat them!

In summary, I suggest reading the book of Leviticus and trying out its diet advice.

Here's the thing: It's hard to know the full truth of something until you try it for yourself. I could give you the best advice and someone else can give you the best advice and it could all make great sense. But if you don't practice this advice, you cheat yourself out of the rewards. The only way to know if something is true (especially when it comes to implementing strategies on what you are consuming) is to do it! Try it and then stick to it. You can't do it some days, then not do it other days and expect to see results. You have to apply it around 80% of the days, and what's going to happen is, in a few months, you're going to start seeing results. After a year, you're going to know this works! Two years in, you'll literally be a new person!

Listen, you've been eating the same way your whole life. What's the harm in substituting fast food and the animals listed in the book of Leviticus with things that are all-natural and perfectly compatible with our genetic makeup?

As I am writing this book, it is 2021. The last two years have been the most unique years of my life, obviously due to COVID-19. Now, more than ever, it is important for all of us to have a strong immune system. This book is not about the details connecting diet to our immune system, but I do feel that it is important to note. Do your own research and be aware of the connection between diet and a strong immune system. Also, do your own research and be aware of the connection between how COVID-19 affects people with a strong immune system compared to how it affects people with a weak immune system.

CHAPTER SIX

THE 80/20 RULE

T HIS CHAPTER IS ABOUT THE 80/20 rule. This rule applies to a lot more than just your diet. It's very basic. If you want to see results in an area of your life, you have to take action and make change eight out of ten days. We're all going to eat food that we really like. Everybody eats food that they know isn't good for them because they really like it. You know, fresh New York Style pizza, the big juicy burger with cheese on it, and ice cream…things like this. If you follow the 80/20 rule and only eat these things two out of ten days, you'll be happy with the results.

Use Flavor to Your Advantage

Now, here's the thing (and I want to make this note right now while I'm thinking about it): All the food that you know is unhealthy for you can be prepared in an all-natural, healthy way. This is where it comes down to understanding how to put flavors together. A chef is just someone who understands how to work with flavors and temperatures. You can make healthy food taste amazing! First of all, I'm a chef. I do not play in the kitchen. If I prepare food, when you taste it, you're going to love me! You're going to fall in love with me! Seriously, that's just the way it is. I don't care what it is. If it's edible and it's good for me, I can make it taste good because I understand flavor combinations.

If you can't cook, all that you have to do is look up recipes on YouTube. YouTube has infinite recipes and step-by-step videos about how to make things taste the way you like them. They have videos on how your favorite restaurant prepares your favorite dish. So, if you just try, you'll start to recognize the pattern of putting things together and what works. You'll begin to recognize which ingredients work with each other, and before you know it, you're going to be cooking like a professional in no time—if you're not already a great cook.

What's super interesting to me is that, after I learned how to make healthy food taste delicious, when I ate the unhealthy food I used to love, it didn't taste good anymore. It's amazing!

80/20

When you decide that you're tired of the way that you look, you're tired of being unhealthy, you're tired of getting sick a few times a year, you're over going to the beach and feeling uncomfortable taking your shirt off, and you're tired of seeing your love handles and belly pouch, then you have to decide that it's time to make some changes! You have to say, "Okay, enough is enough! It's time for me to do what it takes to see results!"

When you make that decision, it may make it easier for you to know that you can use the 80/20 rule. Dedicate eight out of ten days to only eat healthy food. Make the decision that you're not going to eat anything enriched, you're going to remove all fast food, you're going to follow the rules laid out in Leviticus, and you're not going to eat food that's filled with chemicals! Just follow those four simple things eight out of ten days. That's only four out of five days!

When you put something in your mouth, ask yourself these questions and answer them like this: Did I read the ingredients on the back of the pack? (Yes!) Is it chemical-free? (Yes!) Is it not enriched? (Yes!) Is it not fast food? (Yes!) Does it fit the guidelines of the dietary rules that are laid out in the book of Leviticus? (Yes!)

So, four out of five days (every time that you eat) you have to be able to answer yes to those questions. If all checks out, then you can eat that food, and trust me, there are a whole lot of great options! When you do that 80% of the days, 20% of the days you could say, "You know what? I'm going to eat whatever I feel like today. Absolutely anything that I want to eat, I'm going to indulge and I'm going to love it." The beautiful thing about our body is, when we give it time to do what it is designed to do, it will do just that. When we only put natural things into our body, our body automatically gets rid of most (if not all) of the unnatural things in it. So, by eating healthy 80% of the time (which is four days in a row), and then taking a day to eat whatever we feel like, then eating healthy four days in a row again, by the end of that fourth day, we will have gotten rid of most (if not all) of the unhealthy things that we ate on the cheat day.

Right now, I feel that it's important to note that this is a book to start you on a life journey of great health. I personally try to eat good every day. No exceptions, because I believe perfection is attainable. I encourage you to do the same. At the same time, celebrate your daily wins and be gentle with yourself. You've got this!

It's very important to remember, though, that you must have self-accountability. A way to really see how you're doing on your journey to your natural size. One option is to keep a dry erase board calendar on your wall to keep track of what you eat every day. Each night, write down what you ate that day and look at it before you go to sleep. Every day that you eat correctly, and you answered yes to those questions, write a "W" for that day. Give yourself a win! When you eat healthy four days in a row, and you feel like cheating on the fifth day, write down what you ate and still give yourself a win.

However, let's say that you eat healthy three days and unhealthy on the fourth—that is not a win. In other words, write everything down so that you can track your results compared to your actions. Doing this will keep you from forgetting what you may have eaten. It will force you to be honest with yourself. It allows you to congratulate yourself and see your improvements. I highly recommend that you put this into practice.

After four months, you're going to start seeing results. Eight months and you're going to be surprised at how much better you look and feel. A year in, you'll be saying, "WOW! I'm committed to this for life!" Two to three years max (in most cases), you'll be at your natural body size. You will get these results with little to no exercise, watch what I tell you! But just because you can lose weight without exercising doesn't mean that you shouldn't exercise…Which brings me to the next chapter—Emotions.

CHAPTER SEVEN

E.MOTION
(ENERGY IN MOTION)

I CREATED THIS BOOK WITH the intention of helping people lose unwanted weight. However, the real reason is much deeper than that. I want the people who haven't figured out how to be truly happy, healthy, and abundant to understand what needs to be done to attain these things. Happiness is a tricky thing to accomplish because, at the end of the day, the only way that someone can attain this state of being is for them to make a choice within themselves. We all have to do the work to make ourselves happy, healthy, and abundant. For this to happen, we have to look at life through an optimistic lens. We have to see the beauty in the things around us. We have to choose to focus on the good in life rather than the bad. At the same time, this does not mean that we shouldn't be aware of the bad things that are around us either. In fact, we must be aware of the truth. The trick is that optimistic minds can see the good even in the bad. When a bad circumstance arises in an optimistic person's life, they see a lesson and make adjustments. In doing so, they transform "bad" into "good" for themselves.

I've made a choice in life to be like the people that I respect the most. The people that I respect the most are the ones who inspire others to make the choice within themselves to do the work that has to be done in order to see an amazing positive change. This is the type of person that I want to be, and this is the inspiration that I use as I am writing this.

I lost about 100 pounds and I know that it came from a decision that I made to eat differently. I realized that my food choices were the cause of my unhealthy condition. It was something about the way that I felt when my wife poked at my chest and said, "Dang, bae! You getting titties!" It was something about that moment that honestly made me make a choice. It made me look at the reality of my situation and I chose to do something about it. In that moment, I dedicated myself to this new path for life. It was extremely intentional and it came from a place of true dedication. Looking back, I know in my heart today that that was the real moment of success.

In other words, for anything to happen, you have to have a mindset that you are going to do everything that has to get done (for you to get to where you want to go). You have to be excited about it emotionally. You have to know that you want to do what you're about to do, and that you WILL do what you're about to do. Be aware of your emotions and how you feel making this decision, because without a spirit-felt choice of dedication, anything can throw you off your course.

This is basically a how-to book. This is the thing about how-tos, though: they only work if you're in the right emotional state. You have to be looking at your life from the right angle.

Another Diamond

I'm going to drop another name. Elitom Elamin. If you've never heard of this man, I highly suggest that you look him up and do some research. He has a self-named YouTube channel that is extremely interesting. He's what is called a Breatharian. He gets his energy from resources that we have available to us at all times. Resources that we have not been taught how to tap into. Some examples are meditation, conscious breathing, plenty of time in the sunlight, connecting with the ground with our bare feet, yoga, other forms of exercise, and a fun and active lifestyle.

He explains how the letter E in the word Emotion actually stands for energy connected to motion. It stems from ancient knowledge that our emotions are connected to the energy that we put into motion. The more energy that we put into motion, the higher vibrations our emotions will be. Likewise, less energy put into motion results in a lower-vibrational emotion. This is something extremely important to consider. Because even if you lose all of the weight and get down to your natural size, if your emotions are low and you're sad, depressed,

E.MOTION (ENERGY IN MOTION)

aggravated, or angry, does it really matter that you lost the weight that you were looking to lose?

Our emotions are everything in life. Everything that we do, we do because of the emotion that is tied to the activity. We go on vacations because it makes us feel good. We go out to eat for the feeling of the experience. We get into relationships because of the way they make us feel. We watch TV, look at our phones, etc. Literally everything we do is tied to the way it makes us feel.

At the time of writing this, I am 38 years old. I was born in 1983. I remember that when I was a kid, I would go outside and play whenever I got bored. When I was with friends, we would go outside and play. Everything has changed quickly, though. Today, with the advancements of technology, it is so easy to pick up our phone, turn on our smart TV, or get on a video game and be entertained. At the same time, you can be connected with friends literally all over the world and communicate with them via the Internet, as well play a video game with them. I believe it is because of these reasons that many of us spend way too much time indoors.

63

We spend so much time indoors, cooled by a chemically powered air conditioner, blocked off from the rays of the sun—it's no wonder our emotions aren't where we'd like them to be. Just as important as eating the right way, it's important to get outside and get in motion. Do the things that you like outside. Be active!

When you eat naturally, you'll notice that you have energy after you eat. All that you have to do is listen to your energy. Feel your energy when you're done eating. If your energy isn't equal to or higher than it was before you ate (and the hours afterwards), then you know that what you consumed was not naturally compatible with you. Here's the great news, though: Most people think that you have to exercise every day to get the kind of body you want. I know from experience that this is not the case. All you have to do is change the way you eat and you will lose weight. Exercise is simply being in motion. You don't have to go to the gym and push yourself hard until you're sweating to see results. All you have to do is get out of the house and walk. You could also park your car at the back of the parking lot at the grocery store instead of looking for the closest parking spot. You can wake up in the morning and do 20 pushups and 20 sit-ups. If you do this every day, you'll be surprised at the result you'll see overtime. It's really all about consistency and not being stagnant all day. Just get up, move around, and eat right and watch what happens.

Oftentimes, we think that we have to do a lot of exercising in order to lose weight. We've heard quotes like "no pain no gain" and "hard work pays off." Though there's truth in both of these quotes, they are not completely true. My weight loss journey has taught me that the most important factor in maintaining my natural body size is the food I choose to consume. I did not have to exercise every day. I did not have to work hard and sweat the pounds off. When I started eating natural foods and cut the unnatural foods out of my diet, the weight started to come off. That being said, it is also important to keep our bodies in motion. This does not have to be hard work, though. I exercised throughout the day by simply flexing areas of my body. For example, when I'm driving and I see a long straightaway, I make sure to sit up straight and flex my midsection. I flex my stomach and my back and my shoulders, and then I flex my biceps, and then I flex my thighs, and then I flex my calves. When my body is completely flexed, I hold it for about 20 seconds. I do this when I'm standing in a line. I do it when I meditate in the morning while brushing my teeth. Start looking for moments when you can flex your body into the shape that you would like. Flex hard and hold it until you feel yourself getting tired. Then relax. Try this for yourself consistently over time and you'll be surprised with the results.

Remember, this life is really just an experience, so don't beat yourself up every time you make a mistake. If you get off track, it's important to be aware that you're off track, then simply choose to make a correction.

I look at my life journey like it's a game and I'm my only competition. If I'm trying to do something and it doesn't go the way I thought it would, I don't look at it as a loss. I just look for the lesson.

E.MOTION (ENERGY IN MOTION)

Drinking

I started drinking alcohol at an early age in life. The first time I had an alcoholic drink, I was 11 years old. I had a lot of emotions and looking back on it, I think that I was just looking to escape the way that I felt about what I was going through in life. I liked the way alcohol felt; it was something new. However, in reality, it really was just a distraction and it became a bad habit.

Why am I mentioning this? It's very interesting, the effect that alcohol has on our body. Everyone knows that alcohol puts on weight if you drink too much. But what most people don't know is the reason why you put on weight when you drink too much. Alcohol actually slows down our body's fat-burning cells by almost 75%. With only two or three drinks, this effect lasts at least 48 hours. This is important to understand because, most of the time when we drink, we eat something to soak up the alcohol. Now our body is burning the fat from everything we ate 75% slower than if we didn't drink. Knowing this helps in your journey of getting down to your natural body size. I'm not writing this to tell you to

67

never drink but I am saying that it is wise to drink in moderation. Also, when you do decide to drink, be aware of what you're eating within that 48-hour window, as well as what you eat 24 hours prior to drinking. If you eat mostly vegetables and fruits in this time frame, you're making it easier on your body because it will have very little fat to burn off. If you make this change, you will continue to lose weight and you won't get thrown off from your goals because of a bad drinking habit.

While I'm on the topic of drinking I would like to mention a fun fact: Did you know that the water inside of fruits and veggies isn't H_2O? It's actually H_3O_2 and it is called "living water." It is FULL of energy that your body will use to burn fat, ESPECIALLY when you combine it with eating natural foods! So the next time you think about pouring a glass of alcohol I challenge you to juice some watermelon, cucumber, lemon and ginger instead.

CHAPTER EIGHT

THE BREAKFAST, LUNCH AND DINNER LIE

I REMEMBER BEING IN SCHOOL and being taught that breakfast was the most important meal of the day. At the same time, all I really saw as options for breakfast were cereal, pastries, eggs, grits, cheese, hash browns, bacon, sausage, and toast. So let's really look at that. We were taught that breakfast is the most important meal of the day but the choices for breakfast are all unhealthy. I basically never saw vegetables and rarely saw fruit as an option. In actuality, we were taught that the most important thing to do is start your day with an unhealthy meal. We were tricked into believing that being unhealthy is actually important.

This chapter is dedicated to the philosophy of breakfast, lunch, and dinner. I genuinely believe that once you understand the psychological ramifications of eating three meals a day (and how it is connected to why we're so overweight), then you will make the decision to overcome that habit and your life will change forever. Food is big business! Everyone knows this, but I believe that control is even bigger business. There's a very high level of control that is tied to the philosophy of breakfast, lunch, and dinner. Eating three times a day causes us to spend more money than we have to, leading to lack of money (especially for those of us who are not yet financially literate). It also causes us to use more energy than we have to in order to digest the food, creating fatigue and weight gain. Also, tie that to the fact that most of the food we're eating comes out of the grocery store and is laced with chemicals that are detrimental to our body and mind. So, eating like this three times a day not only slows us down physically, but it also slows us down mentally, thus making us easier to be controlled.

Our bodies were not designed to consume so much food. We do not need all of that food for energy. As a matter of fact, eating all of that food is using so much of our body's energy for digestion that it is causing us to be tired and groggy, as well as think slowly.

It's fascinating to me how difficult it is to get over habits that we picked up in childhood. When it comes to the habit of eating three meals per day, I understand that breaking this can be very difficult for a lot of us. The whole reason I wrote this book was to make losing weight as easy as possible. I believe the easiest way to break a habit is to gradually slow down. What worked for me at the beginning was to choose one day out of the week to eat two meals instead of three. Do that for two weeks, and then choose another day of the week to eat twice. Do that for two weeks, and then choose a third day to eat twice. Do that for two weeks, and then choose a fourth day. Repeat this cycle until you have made it to a whole week eating only twice a day. Stick to that for a few months or until you feel like it is easy. Then, choose a day to eat only once and do this for a month. After that, choose another day to eat once (and so on) until eating a full meal only once a day is easy.

Humans are creatures of habit. We do things in cycles. There are cycles all around us in nature. Every day, the sun goes up and goes down. The moon goes up and goes down. Every year, we have spring, summer, fall and winter, so it makes sense that our lifestyles mirror a cycle format. Anything done over and over becomes habitual and easy. So, by eating just one meal less once a week, and slowly removing a meal at a time from your daily habit, it becomes easier to eat less.

Every time that I eat, I ask myself, "Do I really need to eat right now?" Then, I always tell myself that if I don't eat, not only am I treating my body good, but I'm also treating my pockets good. Everybody's different, but this type of self-talk works amazing for me because, even before I make a choice, I'm telling myself the benefits that come along with that choice.

Once it has become a habit to eat only twice a day, you have accomplished a major shift in your life. When you couple eating twice or once a day with eating only healthy foods, you are guaranteed to bring your body back to its natural weight. It's really that simple.

Over time, this choice will lead to a major difference in how you feel and how much you weigh.

Be Aware of Your 30s & Beyond

Time is the ultimate factor in overall truth. I say that because the American food industry is truly pernicious. Google search the definition of pernicious if you don't know what it means. In other words, it's wicked, but you can't tell it's wrong until you've been eating these bad foods consistently over time. Even then, many won't connect the dots. What's scarier is that there's a large percentage of people in America who are unaware of the fact that these chemicals and unnatural foods are the cause of their low energy, being overweight, and getting sick with diseases like cancer. It is truly a tragic situation how slickly evil some of these groups of people who choose to sell chemicals to humans and label them as food are. Real food is natural. It is very important to be aware of the effects of consistently eating these chemicals over time. Toxins compound and continue to negatively affect our lives.

I dedicate this chapter to all of the readers between the ages of 10 and 30. If that's you and you're reading this book, I want you to congratulate yourself! Take a look in the mirror and know that you are truly BRILLIANT! To be so young and to be seeking knowledge on the topic of consumption and health speaks volumes towards your mindset and I have a high level of respect for you. Please reach out to me on social media. I would love to connect with you.

I have to say this: When we're young, our metabolism is high; especially if, genetically, you're skinny and have a lot of skinny people in your family. It's easy to tell yourself that you can eat anything and not get fat and stop thinking about how unhealthy you're being. Some people genetically are super blessed and it's very hard for them to gain weight like other people. But I promise you this, these unnatural foods are affecting you in other ways. They affect you emotionally and spiritually. Down the line (especially after you hit 30 years old), you are more prone two health problems. Most of us know people who have been diagnosed with cancer who are skinny and don't even smoke. These chemicals have harmful effects when consumed consistently over time. This book is not meant to explain the science behind unhealthy foods. There's plenty of literature that exposes this truth. This book is intended to influence you to make a choice to eat naturally for the rest of your life.

Growing up, I was always skinny. I could eat a lot of food and not put on weight. When I went to FIU on a full-ride football scholarship, we had meal plans for the purpose of gaining weight. These meal plans were not based on healthy food. It was based on food that would put weight on you. These meal plans made the horrible eating habit I already had even worse. And after I stopped playing football and stopped exercising, as time passed, I started putting on the pounds. However, everything really started changing after 30 years old. It's almost like everything I'd done up until that point started showing itself ten times faster than before. I know in my spirit that I hit a tipping point due to the decisions I'd been making in regard to what I ate my entire life. All of those years of consuming bad foods accumulated, and when my metabolism started slowing down in my 30s, I blew up like a blimp! When I was young I really didn't think this would happen to me. So, if it happened to me, it can happen to you. It's better to develop a natural, healthy eating habit now while you're young and never have to worry about it than to have to deal with the consequences later in life. A wise mind will understand this.

Comparing Sugar and Iodized Salt to Drugs

There have been experiments done comparing the effects of consuming cooked foods on our brain to the effects of drugs on our brain. Most drugs created in a lab go through a heating process. When things heat up, their chemical composition can change. The studies revealed that our bodies become addicted to these drugs because of the chemical composition change that occurs when the substances are heated. Our bodies crave it. What happens when we stop consuming a lot of these drugs is we go through what we refer to as withdrawal. Amazingly, there have been studies proving that when you consume cooked food, your brain releases the same chemicals as when we consume cooked chemical drugs. These synapses explain that when we stop consuming these cooked chemical drugs, we experience withdrawal. They then go on to compare many of the withdrawal symptoms to what feels like hunger.

In other words, there are studies that prove that what we think is hunger is actually withdrawals from cooked food. I felt that it was important to note this because, when I understood this principle and chose to practice listening to my body and how it felt when I was hungry, then compared it to when I ate raw foods and how hunger felt afterwards, I noticed a major difference. I feel more hungry after eating raw foods, even when my stomach is full. This is my body craving the cooked foods. What's interesting though, is I have more energy after eating raw fruits and vegetables.

The process of heating chemicals up to make drugs is extremely similar to the process used to make iodized salt and processed cane sugar. Choosing to consume these products, regardless of if you're aware of it, is like choosing to consume a drug. Iodized salt and processed cane sugar are pretty much drugs. I encourage you to cut them out of your diet completely. The beautiful thing is all that you have to do is substitute iodized salt for natural sea salt, kosher salt, or Himalayan pink salt; basically any salt that's natural. Also, substitute processed cane sugar with raw organic sugar, natural honey, or any other natural sweeteners instead. All you have to do is substitute the unnatural for the natural and watch how the way you look and feel change right along with it.

I've got some great news for you! Weight loss is actually easy! You don't have to eat a little bit; you just have to eat natural! You can eat until you're full, and you can eat food that tastes absolutely amazing every single day! When you eat natural foods, you'll feel better when you're full compared to how you feel when you're full from foods containing unnatural things.

You should always remember that IT'S A CHOICE TO STAY CONSISTENT! That's the most valuable sentence in this whole book. If you grasp this fact and choose to consistently eat natural at least eight out of ten days for the rest of your life, you will get back to your natural size and feel your optimal energy level, all while being more emotionally sound and stable. Weight loss has been overcomplicated. A lot of people have made a lot of money by complicating things. They've done so to benefit people in the food industry. Unfortunately, there are also organizations in the weight loss industry that also benefit from overcomplicating things in order to keep people coming back seeking answers. The answer is simple! Eat natural! That's all there is to it!

Natural Body Size

I believe that it's very important to include a small section about understanding your natural body size. We are all born with a certain natural body size. This size is different for everybody, but the common theme is the same: All humans are born to be bone and muscle with very little fat. In America, we've been taught that some people are just big-boned and big-boned people have extra fat on their body. This is not the truth. The truth is, if you eat natural, you will never be overweight unless you are gluttonous. But the amazing thing is when you eat natural food for a long period of time, most people do not get the urge to overeat.

Your natural body size is the size of your body after you are fully grown, combined with the intentional choice of a permanent natural diet. Unfortunately, most of us in America have not been eating natural, so we have to spend time reversing the damage caused because of this bad habit. For some people, that might be six months. For some, that might be a year. For others, that might be three to five years. But I promise you this...if you eat natural, consistently following the 80/20 rule, in time you will get down to your natural body size.

CHAPTER NINE

A PERSONAL WORD

W ELL, WHAT DO YOU THINK? After reading all the information in this book and applying logic to what you read, do you feel like you could use this information to get down to your natural body size? If so, there's only one way to find out—now it's time to put it to the test and be blessed!

At the time of writing this book, America has over 70 million adults living with obesity and about 100 million adults that are overweight. My goal is to help at least 1 million people achieve their natural body size by applying the information in this book to their everyday life. For that reason, I ask you to help make this book's easily applied message well-known. I asked that you give this book to anyone you love who could use this information to achieve their natural body size for the rest of their life. Thank you so much for taking the time to help yourself. If you made it to these words, I know you have it in you to achieve your goal. Welcome to a new beginning! As you start to see results from applying this knowledge, please reach out to me and let me know that it's working for you, and let me use your success as inspiration for others. We're all on this journey of life together, and I want you to know I genuinely love you and appreciate your existence! I pray a special prayer for you. I pray that, for the rest of your life, you embody Morality, Healthiness, Happiness, Unity, Financial Literacy in Abundance! You are divine; it's time to eat natural and let your light shine!

MANDATORY CHECKLIST

The following checklist is intended for you to use before you eat any food. By using this checklist, you will keep yourself on the path to your natural body size. As long as you ask yourself these questions before you eat, you will remain at your natural body size once you have achieved it. I pray for that to be for the rest of your life!

For the best results write this checklist down on a piece of paper. There are countless studies to support the fact that when you write down your intentions, the chances of them becoming reality increase drastically.

After writing this checklist down keep the folded piece of paper in your pocket so you can take it out and check it off mentally every time you eat. Do this for 30 days so this list with cement itself in your mind.

☐ It's not fast food

☐ I read the ingredients

☐ It's not enriched

☐ It doesn't have chemical names in the ingredients

☐ It's not pork

☐ If it's an animal, it doesn't drag its belly on the ground like a lizard/reptile

☐ If it comes out of the water, it has scales and fins

☐ If it has hooves, it chews of the cud

(Definition of chew of the cud: They slowly chew their partially digested food over and over again in their mouth before finally swallowing it)

List of Animals with hooves that chew of the cud:

Cattle • Camel • Goat • Giraffe • Deer • Bovid • Sheep • Antelope • Water Buffalo

☐ I don't feel like waiting a while longer before I eat

☐ I didn't choose to fast today

MANDATORY CHECKLIST

If you use this checklist at least eight out of ten days before you eat, you WILL (in time) get down to your natural body size and your energy level/vibration will increase. If you were not already doing these practices, by choosing to focus on and follow this checklist for the rest of your life, your life will drastically change for the better!

ACKNOWLEDGMENTS

In this section I would like to acknowledge the people that helped me in the creation of this book. Everyone on this list, I greatly appreciate for the role they played in guiding me through to the completion of my goals. If you are reading this and have a goal of writing a book, I'll leave contact information in case you would like to reach out to them. Trust me when I say they are all a pleasure to work with!

First, I would like to thank my wife Nicole and mother-in-law Ruthie for being the first two people to edit my book.

To have a wife that makes a house a home is a MAJOR BLESSING. My wife Nicole does just that! She is an AMAZING mom and my best friend. I love you, Bae!

Billionaire PA has helped me in more areas of my life than just this book. To say I'm grateful for our friendship is an understatement. He is truly a world changer! He provided me with valuable information on how to conceptualize structure and write a book—also, how to self-publish, own the rights to the book, and market it!

Contact him on Instagram: @billionairepa

Laura Thomas is the final editor for this book. Not only does she do a great job, but she's a pleasure to work with. Her personality makes it extremely easy to communicate with her through the editing process!

Email contact: laura.thomasj@gmail.com

I hired Tony Shavers to coach me on how to become a best-selling author, and he did just that! He walked me through the process step-by-step, smoothly and efficiently. If you have a goal of becoming a best-selling author, I highly recommend reaching out to him!

Email contact: info@tshavers.com

ACKNOWLEDGMENTS

Jen Henderson at Wild Words Formatting designed my e-book and physical copy. She has a very structured process, and she does wonderful work!

Email contact: wildwordsformatting@gmail.com

Not only did Jamaal Wilcox design the cover of my book, he does designs for my designer clothing brand, Brilliant Minded, as well! This brother brings ideas to life! If you need any graphic design work done, I highly recommend him!

Email contact: malgrfx@gmail.com

Lastly I would like to thank TikTok and Instagram for their platforms. Combined, they've helped me reach millions of people with my content!

My TikTok: @jabez_invests
My Instagram: @jabez_invests

Made in the USA
Middletown, DE
04 September 2024

60316484R00057